fast
Asian

Your Promise of Success

Welcome to the world of Confident Cooking, created for you in
our test Kitchen, where recipes are double-tested by our team
of home economists to achieve a high standard of success.

MURDOCH BOOKS®
Sydney • London • Vancouver • New York

ESSENTIALS

Read on for some time-saving tips, pantry staples and expert advice on how to care for your wok—the most important and versatile piece of equipment for fast and fabulous Asian cooking.

PANTRY

The first step in fast cooking is to have a well-stocked pantry. This keeps your meal options open and cuts down on last-minute shopping expeditions.

ASIAN PANTRY STAPLES

Chinese cooking wine
Coconut cream
Coconut milk
Curry pastes
Dried mushrooms
Fish sauce
Garlic
Ginger
Hoisin sauce
Honey
Mirin
Miso
Noodles
Nuts
Oyster sauce
Peanut oil
Rice
Sambal oelek
Sesame oil
Soft brown sugar or
    palm sugar
Soy sauce
Sweet chilli sauce
Tamarind purée
Vegetable and meat
    stocks

TIME-SAVING TIPS

• Stir-frying is one of the fastest cooking methods. It is also one of the most popular ways of preparing Asian food. The most important thing when stir-frying is to have everything ready before you start cooking. Have all your vegetables chopped into even-sized pieces and any sauces, pastes or liquids measured out.

• Most Asian dishes are served with rice or noodles. Rice usually takes about 15 minutes to cook, so before you start cutting up your vegetables, put the rice on; if it is ready before your meal is, cover and keep warm. Pre-cooked frozen rice is available and can be defrosted in the microwave. Noodle cooking times vary, so time your noodles so that they are cooked when the rest of the meal is ready.

• Buying pre-cut meat will save you time, but be selective as pre-cut meat can be fatty.

• Your wok must be hot before the oil and food are added. This ensures that the cooking time is short and the ingredients, especially meat, will be seared instantly, sealing in the flavour.

EQUIPMENT

A wok is the most essential item for Asian cooking and it can be used for stir-frying, deep-frying or steaming. The other essential utensil is a wok turner or charn—a spade-like scoop ideal for the continuous, fast scooping and turning required when stir-frying. You can buy both at Asian or kitchenware shops.

CARING FOR YOUR WOK

New woks, especially traditional rolled steel ones available from Chinese and Asian stores, are coated with a thin film of lacquer to stop them rusting while on the shelf. This has to be removed before cooking. Fill the wok with cold water and add 2 tablespoons of bicarbonate of soda. Bring to the boil and boil rapidly for 15 minutes. Drain, and scrub off the varnish with a scourer, repeating the process if any of the lacquer coating still remains. Rinse and dry the wok thoroughly.

Place the wok over high heat. Make a wad with a sheet of paper towel and have a small bowl of cooking oil, preferably peanut oil, ready. When the wok is hot, dip the paper in the oil and wipe it over the inner surface of the wok with long-handled tongs—they are safer than rubbing directly onto the surface of the wok with your hands. Repeat with fresh paper until it comes away clean, without any trace of colour. Turn the heat to low and leave for 15 minutes so the wok can absorb the oil. Repeat this process prior to using your wok for the first time.

A properly seasoned wok or non-stick wok should not be scoured on the inside with steel wool. Try not to use detergents as they can damage the seasoning. If you do burn something, you may need to use detergent and even fine steel wool to clean your wok. If this happens, you will need to re-season your wok.

When you have finished cooking and your wok has cooled, wash it with hot water and a soft brush or cloth. Dry it thoroughly before storing in a dry area. If you have a steel wok you should wipe or brush the inside with a very thin layer of oil before storing. Long periods in a dark, warm, airless cupboard can cause the oil coating the wok to turn rancid. Wipe clean with paper towels before use.

NOODLES

Egg noodles: Can be thin (1, 4) or thick (2, 5), flat or round, fresh (1, 2) or dried (4, 5). All egg noodles, fresh or dried, need to be cooked in boiling water before you use them. For broths, always use fresh noodles.

Ramen noodles (3): These noodles are the Japanese interpretation of the Chinese egg noodle—the name ramen means Chinese noodle. These very thin noodles are made from egg and wheat flour. They need to be refrigerated until ready to use. Regular Chinese egg noodles are a good substitute for ramen noodles.

Dried rice vermicelli (6): Packaged in blocks, these thin, translucent whitish noodles need to be soaked in boiling water and well drained before use. They have a slippery texture and absorb the flavours of other foods. When deep fried, they expand and are used as a garnish.

Udon noodles: White Japanese wheat flour noodles, associated with southern Japanese cuisine. They vary in thickness and shape and need to be cooked in boiling water before use. Available fresh (7), instant (8) or dried (9), precooked and shrink-wrapped, but especially good fresh. Mostly used in soups.

Soba noodles (10): A speciality of northern Japan made from buckwheat and/or wheat flour. Eaten hot or cold, they are most commonly available dried.

Fresh rice noodles (11): Available thick or thin, these fresh white rice noodles are steamed and lightly oiled before being sealed and packed.

Fresh rice noodle rolls are made out of the same dough, but are sold in a sheet or roll which can be cut to the desired width.

It is important that both the rice noodles and rolls should be fresh. They will keep for up to two days and are best stored at room temperature as they will become hard and difficult to handle if they are refrigerated.

Hokkien noodles (12): Thick yellow noodles made from egg and wheat flour which are precooked and lightly oiled. They are sold ready to use fresh or vacuum-packed in the refrigerated section of supermarkets and Asian food stores. Hokkien noodles are used in many Asian cuisines.

Mung bean thread vermicelli (13): Also known as cellophane or glass noodles, these flat or thread-like, translucent noodles are made from mung beans and sold packaged in blocks. They are very hard to cut but soften when cooked or soaked in boiling water. When fried in oil, either straight from the packet or after being soaked and drained, they puff up.

Rice stick noodles: These translucent, flat dried noodles can be wide (14) or slender (15) They are used in stir-fries as well as soups and salads. They are packaged in bundles and need to be soaked in warm water before use.

INGREDIENTS

BEAN SAUCE: Made from crushed soy beans, barley, sesame oil, sugar and salt. Do not confuse with ground bean sauce or chilli bean paste which are sometimes labelled as bean sauce—read the ingredients list to make sure you are buying the right thing.

BLACK BEANS: A type of soy bean, available dried, fermented, salted and canned in brine. Do not confuse with turtle beans used in South American cooking, which can also be called black beans.

CHINESE BROCCOLI (gai larn): A green vegetable with slightly leathery leaves and thick, green stalks. Both the leaves and stalks are used.

CHINESE FIVE SPICE: A common seasoning used in Chinese cooking, containing star anise, fennel, cinnamon, cloves and Sichuan pepper.

CHINESE RICE WINE OR COOKING WINE (Shao Hsing): Made from glutinous rice in Shao Hsing in southern China. This amber-coloured liquid has a rich sweetish taste. Use dry sherry if unavailable.

COCONUT CREAM AND MILK: Extracted from the flesh of fresh coconuts. The cream is thick and almost spreadable. The milk is extracted after the cream has been pressed out and is thinner.

CRISP FRIED SHALLOTS: Deep-fried red Asian shallot flakes used as a garnish in South-east Asia. Available from Asian food stores in packets or tubs. Store in the freezer.

DASHI: A basic Japanese stock made with dried kelp and dried bonito (a fish). Available in flakes or granules. Add hot water to make a stock.

DRIED MUSHROOMS: One of the most popular dried mushrooms is shiitake. Dried Chinese mushrooms are also popular (whole or sliced).

ENOKI MUSHROOMS: Tiny white Japanese mushrooms on long, thin stalks growing in clumps. Do not cook for long.

FISH SAUCE: A brown, salty sauce with a 'fishy' smell. Small fish are salted and fermented—the run off is fish sauce.

GALANGAL: A rhizome available fresh, sliced in brine, dried slices in packets, and powdered. Soak the dried slices in warm water for 30 minutes before use.

HOISIN SAUCE: A sweet, thick sauce made from fermented soy beans flavoured with garlic and five-spice powder.

KAFFIR LIME LEAVES: Fragrant leaves from the kaffir lime tree. The dark green, double leaves are available fresh or dried.

KECAP MANIS: A thick, sweet soy sauce used in Indonesian and Malaysian cuisines. If unavailable, use soy sauce sweetened with a little soft brown sugar.

LAP CHOONG (Chinese sausage): Dried sausages with a sweetish smoky flavour. Made of pork meat, they are not to be confused with a similar sausage, gum gun yuen, which contains duck and pork liver. Do not eat raw: stir-fry or steam. Keeps for 3 weeks in plastic wrap in the fridge. Can be frozen.

MIRIN: A mild, low-alcohol form of sake, this rice cooking wine lends a sweetness to sauces, grilled dishes and glazes. Often used in Japanese cuisine.

MISO: A protein-rich paste made from cooked, mashed, salted, fermented soy beans and grains, usually barley or rice. It varies in colour, texture and saltiness. The colour can range from brown, light brown, yellow and white. The darker pastes have been matured longer and are saltier and more pungent than the lighter ones.

MIZUNA: A Japanese, leafy vegetable with juicy well-flavoured leaves. Suitable for salads and stir-fries.

NORI: Dried seaweed that comes in sheets or soft shreds, plain or roasted. Quick toasting over a naked flame freshens the nori and produces a nutty flavour. The sheets are usually used for making sushi rolls.

PALM SUGAR: A rich, aromatic sugar from the boiled down sap of several kinds of palm tree. Thai palm sugar is lighter in colour and more refined than the Indonesian or Malay versions. If unavailable, use soft brown sugar.

PICKLED GINGER: Fresh, thin, pink slices of ginger preserved in brine. Used in Japanese rice dishes and as a garnish. A good palate cleanser with a very sharp flavour.

RICE PAPER WRAPPERS: These round or square thin sheets made from rice flour, water and salt are bought dried in sealed packets and will keep indefinitely, but handle with care as they are very brittle. Briefly soak them in warm water before use.

RICE VINEGAR: A clear, pale yellow, mild and sweet-tasting vinegar made from rice.

SAKE: A Japanese wine made by fermenting cooked ground rice mash, used for cooking and drinking, depending on the grade.

SAMBAL OELEK: A hot paste made from fresh red chillies, mashed and mixed with salt and vinegar or tamarind.

SESAME OIL: A concentrated oil from toasted white sesame seeds used sparingly for flavour. Keep in a cool, dark place.

SHRIMP PASTE: A pungent paste made from fermented prawns. It can be pink and soft or dark and hard. Keep wrapped in plastic and stored in the refrigerator in an airtight container to reduce the smell. Always fry or roast before using.

SICHUAN PEPPERCORNS: A Chinese spice made from the red berries of the prickly ash tree and sold whole or ground. The flavour is woody and it has a strong, hot, numbing aftertaste. Often the powder is dry-fried to bring out the flavours.

STAR ANISE: A star-shaped Chinese fruit made up of eight segments. They are sun-dried until hard and brown and have a pronounced aniseed aroma and sweet aniseed flavour.

STRAW MUSHROOMS: These small, unopened, button-shaped mushrooms are very high in protein. They are most commonly found canned—drain and rinse them well before using.

TAMARIND: A large, brown, bean-like pod with a fruity, tart flavour. Available as a dried shelled fruit, a block of compressed pulp (usually with seeds), or as a purée or concentrate. It is often added to curries.

THAI BASIL: The leaves of Thai basil are smaller and darker than regular basil and are used extensively in Asian cooking. The stems and younger leaves have a purplish tinge and the flowers are pink. The flavour of the leaves is a blend of aniseed and cloves.

TOFU (Clockwise from top.) Once opened, tofu (except fried puffs) will keep for up to 5 days in the refrigerator covered in water which should be changed every 2 days. Fried tofu puffs: Tofu cubes which are deep-fried until puffed and golden. Can be frozen. Silken firm tofu: It has a smooth, custard-like texture and is quite firm. When blended, the texture is similar to a heavy cream or yoghurt. Can be deep-fried and used in soups.
Silken tofu: With a custard-like texture, when blended the texture is similar to cream and typically acts as a substitute for milk, cream, mayonnaise and eggs. Due to its delicate consistency, silken tofu does not stir-fry well as it breaks down easily when handled. Often used cubed in soups. Firm tofu: holds its shape when cooking. Suitable for stir-frying, pan-frying and baking. Can be crumbled, sliced and cubed. Often used as a meat substitute. Blending is not recommended.

WASABI PASTE: A pungent paste often used as an accompaniment in Japanese food. Most often, wasabi paste is made from horseradish powder, mustard powder and other ingredients for colour. It is extremely hot, so use sparingly. Also available as a powder.

WATER CHESTNUTS: Small, rounded, crisp vegetables, usually sold canned. They give a crunchy texture to many Asian dishes. Any unused water chestnuts will keep fresh for four days if immersed in water in the fridge; change the water daily.

WATER SPINACH: A leafy vegetable with long, pointed leaves and pale, hollow stems.

FAST ASIAN MEALS

Now there's no need to resort to the local take-away for an easy night in with the authentic taste of Asia—your favourite soups, salads, stir-fries and curries are all here and are ready to eat in just 30 minutes. Stick with the classics or explore new tastes from the Asian region without having to leave your kitchen.

THAI-STYLE CHICKEN AND COCONUT SOUP
Ready to eat in 30 minutes
Serves 4

2 stems lemon grass, white part finely chopped, stem ends reserved and halved
6 cloves garlic, chopped
3 red Asian shallots, chopped
8 black peppercorns
1 teaspoon ready-made red curry paste
1 cup (250 ml) coconut cream
400 ml coconut milk
400 ml chicken stock
2 1/2 tablespoons thinly sliced fresh galangal
7 kaffir lime leaves, shredded
400 g chicken breast fillets or thigh fillets, thinly sliced
2 tablespoons lime juice
2 tablespoons fish sauce
1 teaspoon grated palm sugar
3 tablespoons fresh coriander leaves
1 small fresh red chilli, thinly sliced

1 Process the chopped lemon grass, garlic, shallots, peppercorns and curry paste in a food processor to a paste.
2 Heat a wok over low heat, add the coconut cream, increase the heat to high and bring to the boil. Add the paste and cook, stirring, for 5 minutes. Add the coconut milk and stock, return to the boil and add the galangal, the lime leaves and reserved lemon grass stems. Reduce the heat and simmer for 5 minutes.
3 Add the chicken and simmer for 8 minutes, or until cooked. Stir in the lime juice, fish sauce, palm sugar, coriander leaves and chilli. Serve immediately.

Nutrition per serve: Fat 36.5 g; Protein 28 g; Carbohydrate 10 g; Dietary Fibre 4.5 g; Cholesterol 50 mg; 2000 kJ (475 Cal)

Thai-style chicken and coconut soup

SESAME TUNA STEAKS WITH NORI RICE
Ready to eat in 30 minutes
Serves 4

4 x 200 g tuna steaks
3/4 cup (115 g) sesame
  seeds
1 cup (200 g) medium-grain
  rice
2 1/2 tablespoons rice wine
  vinegar
1 tablespoon mirin
1 teaspoon sugar
1 sheet nori, finely shredded
1/4 cup (60 ml) peanut oil
1/2 cup (125 g) Japanese or
  whole-egg mayonnaise
2 teaspoons wasabi paste
pickled ginger, to serve

1 Coat the tuna steaks in the sesame seeds, pressing down to coat well. Refrigerate until needed.
2 Wash the rice until the water runs clear, then place in a saucepan with 2 cups (500 ml) water. Bring to the boil, then reduce the heat to as low as possible and cook, covered, for 10–12 minutes. Turn off the heat and leave, covered, for 5 minutes. While hot, pour on the combined rice wine vinegar, mirin, sugar and 1/4 teaspoon salt. Stir with a fork to separate the grains and fold in the shredded nori. Keep warm.
3 Heat the oil in a large frying pan, add the tuna and cook for 1–2 minutes on each side, or until the sesame seeds are crisp and golden. The tuna should still be a little pink in the middle. Drain on paper towels.
4 Spoon the rice into lightly greased 1/2 cup (125 ml) ramekins, pressing down lightly, then invert onto each plate and remove the ramekin. Combine the mayonnaise and wasabi paste in a small bowl. Serve the tuna alongside the rice mould with some wasabi mayonnaise on the side and garnished with pickled ginger, if desired.

Nutrition per serve: Fat 52 g; Protein 60 g; Carbohydrate 48 g; Dietary Fibre 5 g; Cholesterol 82.5 mg; 3775 kJ (900 Cal)

PRAWN LAKSA
Ready to eat in 25 minutes
Serves 4

250 g dried rice vermicelli
1 tablespoon peanut oil
1/4 cup (60 g) good-quality
  laksa paste
3 cups (750 ml) vegetable
  stock
400 ml coconut milk
500 g peeled and deveined,
  raw medium prawns with
  tails intact (see Note)
3 tablespoons chopped
  fresh coriander leaves
75 g fried tofu puffs, cut into
  5 mm wide matchsticks
1 cup (90 g) bean sprouts
1/4 cup (40 g) crushed
  peanuts
fresh coriander leaves,
  to garnish
lime wedges (optional)

1 Put the vermicelli in a large heatproof bowl, cover with boiling water and leave for 10 minutes, then drain.
2 Heat a wok over high heat, add the oil and swirl to coat. Add the laksa paste and stir-fry for 1 minute. Add the stock and bring to the boil, then reduce the heat, add the coconut milk and simmer for 2 minutes. Add the prawns and cook for 2–3 minutes, or until they change colour, then add the coriander, tofu and 1/4 teaspoon salt, and cook for 2 minutes.
3 Run the noodles under hot water to separate, then divide among four deep bowls. Top with bean sprouts, then ladle in the soup. Garnish with the crushed peanuts and coriander leaves. Serve with lime wedges.

Nutrition per serve: Fat 38.5 g; Protein 35 g; Carbohydrate 62 g; Dietary Fibre 5 g; Cholesterol 186.5 mg; 3060 kJ (730 Cal)

Note: If you can't buy peeled raw prawns, buy 1 kg and peel them yourself. This will add 15 minutes to your preparation time.

Sesame tuna steaks with nori rice (top), and Prawn laksa

CHINESE FRIED RICE

Ready to eat in 25 minutes
Serves 4–6

1/4 cup (60 ml) oil
2 eggs, lightly beaten
1 carrot, thinly sliced
1 red capsicum, diced
6 fresh baby corn, sliced
2 cloves garlic, crushed
1/2 cup (80 g) frozen peas
100 g lap choong sausages, sliced on the diagonal
1.5 kg frozen cooked long-grain rice, thawed (see Note)
3 spring onions, thinly sliced
31/2 tablespoons soy sauce
2 teaspoons sugar
2 teaspoons sesame oil

1 Heat a wok or large frying pan over high heat, add 1 tablespoon of the oil and swirl to coat. Add the egg and swirl to distribute evenly. Cook for 1–2 minutes, or until golden, then turn and cook the other side. Remove, leave until cool enough to handle, then roll up and thinly slice.
2 Heat the remaining oil over high heat, add the carrot and stir-fry for 1 minute, then add the capsicum and cook for another minute. Finally, add the corn, garlic, peas and sausage and stir-fry for 1 minute.
3 Add the rice, spring onion and omelette, and mix, separating the rice grains. Stir over medium heat for 3–4 minutes, or until the rice is warmed through. Stir in the soy sauce, sugar and sesame oil, and toss. Serve hot.

Nutrition per serve (6): Fat 18 g; Protein 15 g; Carbohydrate 95 g; Dietary Fibre 5 g; Cholesterol 86 mg; 2525 kJ (605 Cal)

Note: If you are not using frozen rice, you will need to cook 3 cups (600 g) rice, then cool.

Variation: Instead of lap choong sausage, try Chinese barbecue pork, sliced ham or prawns.

VIETNAMESE CHICKEN SALAD

Ready to eat in 30 minutes
Serves 4

400 g chicken breast fillets
1 stem lemon grass, white part only, finely chopped
1 tablespoon fish sauce
2 teaspoons sugar
2 tablespoons lime juice
11/2 tablespoons sweet chilli sauce
200 g Chinese cabbage (wom buk), thinly sliced
1 carrot, cut into ribbons with a vegetable peeler
1/2 small red onion, sliced
1/2 cup (15 g) fresh coriander leaves
1/2 cup (25 g) roughly chopped fresh mint
2 tablespoons fresh coriander leaves, extra
2 tablespoons chopped peanuts
1 tablespoon crisp fried shallots

1 Place the chicken and lemon grass in a deep frying pan of lightly salted water. Bring to the boil, then reduce the heat and simmer gently for 8–10 minutes, or until the chicken is just cooked through. Drain and keep warm.
2 Place the fish sauce, sugar, lime juice and sweet chilli sauce in a small saucepan and stir over medium heat for 1 minute, or until the sugar has dissolved. Remove from the heat.
3 Place the cabbage, carrot, onion, coriander and mint in a large bowl, and toss together well. Pour on three-quarters of the warmed dressing, toss to combine and transfer to a serving platter.
4 Slice the chicken thinly on the diagonal, arrange over the top of the salad and drizzle with the remaining dressing. Garnish with the extra coriander leaves, chopped peanuts and crisp fried shallots. Serve immediately.

Nutrition per serve: Fat 8.5 g; Protein 25 g; Carbohydrate 7 g; Dietary Fibre 2.5 g; Cholesterol 66 mg; 850 kJ (205 Cal)

Variation: Instead of Chinese cabbage, a large green pawpaw may be used. Remove the skin and finely shred the fruit.

Chinese fried rice (top), and Vietnamese chicken salad

JAPANESE-STYLE STEAK SALAD

Ready to eat in 20 minutes
Serves 4

750 g rump steak
3 teaspoons oil
3 teaspoons wasabi paste
1/2 teaspoon Dijon mustard
1 teaspoon grated fresh
    ginger
2 tablespoons rice wine
    vinegar
3 tablespoons pickled
    ginger, plus 1 tablespoon
    pickling liquid
2 tablespoons sesame oil
1/4 cup (60 ml) oil, extra
100 g baby spinach leaves
100 g mizuna or watercress,
    trimmed
4 radishes, thinly sliced
1 Lebanese cucumber,
    peeled and cut into
    ribbons with a vegetable
    peeler
1/4 cup (40 g) sesame
    seeds, toasted

1 Generously season
the steak with salt and
freshly cracked black
pepper. Heat the oil in a
large frying pan or heat
a barbecue plate to very
hot. Add the steak and
cook for 2–3 minutes
on each side, or until
browned. Remove and
leave to rest, covered,
for 5 minutes.
2 Place the wasabi
paste, mustard, ginger,
rice wine vinegar,
pickled ginger, pickling
liquid and 1/2 teaspoon
salt in a large bowl and
whisk together. Whisk
in the oils, then add the
spinach, mizuna, radish
and cucumber to the
bowl and toss to coat.
3 Slice the steak across
the grain into thin strips.
Divide the salad among
four serving plates,
top with the beef slices
and sprinkle with
sesame seeds. Serve
immediately.

Nutrition per serve: Fat 32 g;
Protein 45 g; Carbohydrate 2 g;
Dietary Fibre 3 g; Cholesterol
121 mg; 1980 kJ (475 Cal)

MISO SOUP WITH CHICKEN AND UDON NOODLES

Ready to eat in 30 minutes
Serves 4–6

8 dried shiitake mushrooms
600 g chicken breast fillets,
    cut into 1.5 cm thick strips
1/4 cup (60 g) white miso
    paste
2 teaspoons dashi granules
1 tablespoon wakame flakes
    or other seaweed (see
    Note)
300 g baby bok choy,
    halved lengthways
400 g fresh Udon noodles
150 g silken firm tofu, cut
    into 1 cm cubes
3 spring onions, sliced
    diagonally

1 Soak the mushrooms
in 1 cup (250 ml) boiling
water for 20 minutes.
Drain, reserving the
liquid; discard the stalks
and thinly slice the caps.
2 Pour 2 litres water
into a saucepan and
bring to the boil, then
reduce the heat and
simmer. Add the
chicken and cook for
2–3 minutes, or until
almost cooked through.
3 Add the mushrooms
and cook for 1 minute,
then add the miso paste,
dashi granules, wakame
and reserved mushroom
liquid. Stir to dissolve
the dashi and miso paste.
Do not boil.
4 Add the bok choy
halves and simmer for
1 minute, or until
beginning to wilt, then
add the noodles and
simmer for a further
2 minutes. Gently stir in
the tofu and ladle the
hot soup into large
serving bowls. Garnish
with the sliced spring
onion.

Nutrition per serve (6): Fat 10 g;
Protein 35 g; Carbohydrate 26 g;
Dietary Fibre 4 g; Cholesterol
79 mg; 1385 kJ (330 Cal)

Note: Wakame is a curly-leafed,
brown algae with a mild
vegetable taste and a soft
texture. It can be used in salads
or can be boiled and served up
like a vegetable. Use a small
amount as it swells by about ten
times after being cooked.

Japanese-style steak salad
(top), and Miso soup with
chicken and Udon noodles

CHICKEN WITH THAI BASIL, CHILLI AND CASHEWS

Ready to eat in 30 minutes
Serves 4

750 g chicken breast or
    thigh fillets, cut into strips
2 stems lemon grass, white
    part only, finely chopped
3 small fresh red chillies,
    seeded and finely chopped
4 cloves garlic, crushed
1 tablespoon finely chopped
    fresh ginger
2 fresh coriander roots, finely
    chopped
2 tablespoons oil
100 g cashews
1 1/2 tablespoons lime juice
2 tablespoons fish sauce
1 1/2 tablespoons shaved
    palm sugar or soft brown
    sugar
2 cups (60 g) lightly packed
    fresh Thai basil
2 teaspoons cornflour mixed
    with 1 tablespoon water

1 Place the chicken in a large bowl with the lemon grass, chilli, garlic, ginger and coriander root. Mix together well.
2 Heat a wok over medium heat, add 1 teaspoon of the oil and swirl to coat the surface of the wok. Add the cashews and cook for 1 minute, or until lightly golden. Remove and drain on paper towels.

3 Heat the remaining oil in the wok, add the chicken in batches and stir-fry over medium heat for 4–5 minutes, or until browned. Return the chicken to the wok.
4 Stir in the lime juice, fish sauce, palm sugar and basil, and cook for 30–60 seconds, or until the basil just begins to wilt. Add the cornflour mixture and stir until the mixture thickens slightly. Stir in the cashews and serve with steamed rice.

Nutrition per serve: Fat 32.5 g; Protein 46 g; Carbohydrate 15 g; Dietary Fibre 2.5 g; Cholesterol 123.5 mg; 2220 kJ (530 Cal)

LEMON GRASS PRAWNS

Ready to eat in 20 minutes
Serves 4

5 stems lemon grass, white
    part only, finely chopped
2 cloves garlic, chopped
3 teaspoons grated fresh
    ginger
2 tablespoons oil
1 red onion or 5 red Asian
    shallots, cut into wedges
500 g peeled and deveined,
    raw medium prawns with
    tails intact (see Note)
1 tablespoon lime juice
2 kaffir lime leaves,
    shredded
2 tablespoons fish sauce
2 tablespoons grated light
    palm sugar
fresh coriander leaves, to
    garnish

1 Place the lemon grass, garlic, ginger and 1 tablespoon of the oil in a food processor or spice grinder, and process to a smooth paste.
2 Heat a wok over high heat, add the remaining oil and swirl to coat. Add the onion and stir-fry over high heat for 1 minute, then add the paste and stir-fry for a further 2 minutes, or until fragrant.
3 Add the prawns to the wok, cook for 2 minutes, and stir in the combined lime juice, lime leaves, fish sauce, palm sugar and 1 1/2 tablespoons water. Cook for another 2 minutes, or until the sugar has completely dissolved. Garnish with the coriander leaves and serve with steamed rice.

Nutrition per serve: Fat 10 g; Protein 27 g; Carbohydrate 8 g; Dietary Fibre 0.5 g; Cholesterol 186.5 mg; 955 kJ (230 Cal)

Note: If you can't buy peeled raw prawns, buy 1 kg and peel them yourself. This will add 15 minutes to your preparation time.

Chicken with Thai basil, chilli and cashews (top) and Lemon grass prawns

NORI OMELETTE WITH STIR-FRIED VEGETABLES

Ready to eat in 30 minutes
Serves 4

8 eggs
18 cm x 10 cm sheet nori
1/4 cup (60 ml) oil
1 clove garlic, crushed
3 teaspoons finely grated fresh ginger
1 carrot, cut into thick matchsticks
2 zucchini, halved lengthways, sliced on the diagonal
200 g mix of Swiss brown, enoki and oyster mushrooms, larger ones sliced
1 tablespoon Japanese soy sauce
1 tablespoon mirin
2 teaspoons yellow miso paste

1 Lightly beat the eggs. Roll the nori up tightly and snip with scissors into very fine strips. Add to the eggs and season to taste with salt and cracked black pepper.
2 Heat a wok over high heat, add 2 teaspoons of the oil and swirl to coat the side of the wok. Add 1/3 cup (80 ml) of the egg mixture and swirl to coat the base of the wok. Cook for 2 minutes, or until set, then turn over and cook the other side for 1 minute. Remove and keep warm. Repeat with the remaining mixture, adding another 2 teaspoons of the oil each time, to make four omelettes.
3 Heat the remaining oil in the wok, add the garlic and ginger and stir-fry for 1 minute. Add the carrot, zucchini and mushrooms in two batches and stir-fry for 3 minutes, or until softened. Return all the vegetables to the wok. Add the soy sauce, mirin and miso paste, and simmer for 1 minute. Divide the vegetables evenly among the omelettes, roll them up and serve immediately with rice.

Nutrition per serve: Fat 24.5 g; Protein 17 g; Carbohydrate 4 g; Dietary Fibre 5 g; Cholesterol 375 mg; 1240 kJ (295 Cal)

SOY-GLAZED SALMON

Ready to eat in 30 minutes
Serves 4

1/2 cup (125 ml) soy sauce
2 tablespoons honey
1 tablespoon grated fresh ginger
1/3 cup (80 ml) lime juice
4 x 180 g salmon fillets
2 tablespoons peanut oil
2 cloves garlic, crushed
150 g snow peas, trimmed
1 red capsicum, sliced
1 tablespoon soy sauce, extra
300 g English spinach leaves

1 Whisk together the soy sauce, honey, ginger and lime juice. Place the salmon fillets in a shallow non-metallic dish and pour on the marinade. Rub the marinade into both sides of the fillets and leave for 8 minutes.
2 Cook the salmon fillets under a hot grill, basting with the marinade, for 8–10 minutes on one side only, or until the fish cooks through and is blackened on top.
3 Meanwhile, heat a wok over medium heat, add the oil and swirl to coat. Add the garlic and stir-fry for 30 seconds without browning. Increase the heat and add the snow peas and capsicum and stir-fry for 2 minutes. Add the extra soy sauce and the spinach and stir-fry for 1–2 minutes, or until the spinach has wilted. Serve the salmon on a bed of the vegetables.

Nutrition per serve: Fat 23 g; Protein 41 g; Carbohydrate 17 g; Dietary Fibre 3.5 g; Cholesterol 93.5 mg; 1805 kJ (430 Cal)

Nori omelette with stir-fried vegetables (top), and Soy-glazed salmon

CHINESE PORK WITH ASIAN COLESLAW

Ready to eat in 15 minutes
Serves 4

250 g Chinese roasted pork
2 tablespoons light soy
    sauce
1 1/2 tablespoons mirin
1/2 teaspoon sesame oil
2 teaspoons lime juice
2 teaspoons sugar
3 cups (135 g) Chinese
    cabbage (wom buk),
    finely shredded
1 cup (90 g) bean sprouts
1 large carrot, grated
3 tablespoons fresh
    coriander leaves
3 spring onions, thinly sliced
lime wedges, to serve

1 Thinly slice the roasted pork. Place the soy sauce, mirin, sesame oil, lime juice and sugar in a bowl and mix well.
2 Place the cabbage, bean sprouts, carrot, coriander leaves and spring onion in a large bowl and toss to combine. Pour on the dressing and toss through. Divide the coleslaw among four serving plates, top with the pork and serve with lime wedges.

Nutrition per serve: Fat 3 g;
Protein 22 g; Carbohydrate 4.5 g;
Dietary Fibre 2 g; Cholesterol
80 mg; 555 kJ (135 Cal)

Chinese pork with Asian coleslaw (top), and Fish cakes with Thai-style salad

FISH CAKES WITH THAI-STYLE SALAD

Ready to eat in 30 minutes
Serves 4

400 g white fish fillets (e.g.
    snapper or perch),
    trimmed and cubed
2 tablespoons ready-made
    red curry paste
2 kaffir lime leaves, finely
    shredded
2 tablespoons coconut
    cream
1 egg white
140 g green beans,
    blanched
2 spring onions, finely
    chopped, green part only
100 g snow peas, blanched
    and sliced
1/2 red capsicum, sliced
1 Lebanese cucumber,
    seeded, sliced
2 spring onions, extra,
    sliced diagonally
1/2 cup (15 g) fresh
    coriander leaves
1/3 cup (80 ml) rice or white
    wine vinegar
1 tablespoon sugar
1 teaspoon dried red chilli
    flakes
1/4 cup (60 ml) coconut
    cream, extra
1 small fresh red chilli,
    seeded, julienned

1 Preheat the oven to moderately hot 200°C (400°F/Gas 6). Place the fish pieces, curry paste, kaffir lime leaves, coconut cream and egg white in a food processor, and process until combined. Transfer to a bowl.

2 Cut 40 g of the green beans into thin rounds and fold through the fish mixture with the finely chopped spring onion.
3 Divide the mixture into 12 equal portions with wetted hands. Lightly grease a mini muffin tray. Flatten the fish mixture into patties to fit the tin and bake for 6–8 minutes.
4 Meanwhile, slice the remaining green beans lengthways and place in a bowl with the snow peas, capsicum, cucumber, extra spring onion and coriander.
5 Place the vinegar and sugar in a saucepan, and stir over medium heat for 1 minute, or until the sugar has dissolved. Remove from the heat, stir in the chilli flakes and leave to cool.
6 Divide the salad and fish cakes among four serving plates and drizzle with the dressing. Top each fish cake with a little coconut cream and garnish with the julienned chilli.

Nutrition per serve: Fat 11 g;
Protein 24 g; Carbohydrate 7.5 g;
Dietary Fibre 3 g; Cholesterol
59 mg; 940 kJ (225 Cal)

PRAWN AND SOBA NOODLE SALAD
Ready to eat in 20 minutes
Serves 4

1 tablespoon finely chopped fresh ginger
1 clove garlic, finely chopped
1/3 cup (80 ml) rice wine vinegar
1 teaspoon sugar
2 teaspoons sesame oil
1/3 cup (80 ml) Japanese or light soy sauce
250 g dried soba noodles
400 g cooked, peeled and deveined medium prawns (see Note)
1 small red capsicum, julienned
4 spring onions, sliced diagonally
1 tablespoon sesame seeds, toasted

1 Place the ginger, garlic, vinegar, sugar, sesame oil, soy sauce and 1/4 teaspoon freshly ground black pepper and 1/2 teaspoon salt in a small bowl and combine well.
2 Bring a large saucepan of lightly salted water to the boil. Add the noodles and cook for 4–5 minutes, or until just tender. Rinse under cold water, drain and place in a large bowl with the prawns, capsicum, spring onion and dressing. Toss to combine and season to taste with salt and freshly ground black pepper. Evenly divide the salad among four serving bowls and sprinkle with the toasted sesame seeds.

Nutrition per serve: Fat 16 g; Protein 26 g; Carbohydrate 37 g; Dietary Fibre 5.5 g; Cholesterol 192 mg; 1670 kJ (400 Cal)

Note: If you can't buy peeled cooked prawns, buy 800 g and peel them yourself. This will add about 15 minutes to your preparation time.

VEGETABLE RAMEN
Ready to eat in 30 minutes
Serves 6

375 g fresh ramen noodles
1 tablespoon oil
1 tablespoon finely chopped fresh ginger
2 cloves garlic, crushed
150 g oyster mushrooms, halved
1 small zucchini, sliced into thin rounds
1 leek, white and light green part, halved lengthways and thinly sliced
100 g snow peas, halved diagonally
100 g fried tofu puffs, cut into matchsticks
1.25 litres vegetable stock
1 1/2 tablespoons white miso paste
2 tablespoons light soy sauce
1 tablespoon mirin
1 cup (90 g) bean sprouts
1 teaspoon sesame oil
4 spring onions, thinly sliced
100 g enoki mushrooms

1 Bring a large saucepan of lightly salted water to the boil. Add the noodles and cook, stirring to prevent sticking, for 4 minutes, or until just tender. Drain and rinse under cold running water.
2 Heat the oil in a large saucepan over medium heat, add the ginger, crushed garlic, oyster mushrooms, zucchini, leek, snow peas and tofu puffs, and stir-fry for 2 minutes. Add the stock and 300 ml water and bring to the boil, then reduce the heat and simmer. Stir in the miso, soy sauce and mirin until heated through. Do not boil. Stir in the bean sprouts and sesame oil.
3 Place the noodles in the bottom of six serving bowls, then pour in the soup. Garnish with the spring onion and enoki mushrooms.

Nutrition per serve: Fat 6.5 g; Protein 13 g; Carbohydrate 38 g; Dietary Fibre 5 g; Cholesterol 8.5 mg; 1090 kJ (260 Cal)

Prawn and soba noodle salad (top), and Vegetable ramen

VIETNAMESE DUCK RICE PAPER ROLLS

Ready to eat in 20 minutes
Serves 4 as a light meal

16 x 22 cm round
    Vietnamese rice paper
    wrappers
1 whole Chinese roast duck,
    meat removed from the
    bones and chopped
    (see Note)
1 telegraph cucumber
150 g bean sprouts

Sauce
1 tablespoon hoisin sauce
2 teaspoons chilli sauce
1 tablespoon plum sauce

1 Half-fill a large bowl with warm water and a second bowl with cold water. Dip each wrapper into the warm water for 10 seconds and then into the cold water. Drain on paper towels and stack on a serving plate with greaseproof paper between each wrapper.
2 Remove any remaining bones from the duck and shred the meat. Place in a serving dish. Cut the cucumber in half lengthways and scrape out the seeds. Cut the cucumber into 1 cm x 6 cm strips. Place in a serving dish. Put the bean sprouts in a separate serving dish. Combine the sauce ingredients and place in a small dish.
3 Invite your guests to assemble their rolls at the table. To assemble, spread a little sauce onto the rice paper wrapper, then arrange the filling ingredients on the top half of the wrapper. Fold over the bottom edge then roll up, tucking in the sides.

Nutrition per serve: Fat 7.5 g; Protein 20 g; Carbohydrate 25 g; Dietary Fibre 2 g; Cholesterol 103 mg; 1020 kJ (245 Cal)

Note: Chinese roast duck is available from Chinese barbecue outlets.

MUSSELS WITH BLACK BEANS AND CORIANDER

Ready to eat in 25 minutes
Serves 4

1.5 kg black mussels
1 tablespoon peanut oil
2 tablespoons canned,
    salted black beans, rinsed
    and mashed
2 cloves garlic, finely
    chopped
1 teaspoon finely chopped
    fresh ginger
2 long fresh red chillies,
    seeded and finely chopped
1 tablespoon finely chopped
    fresh coriander root
1/4 cup (60 ml) Chinese rice
    wine or dry sherry
2 tablespoons lime juice
2 teaspoons sugar
1/2 cup (15 g) fresh
    coriander leaves, roughly
    chopped

1 Scrub the mussels with a stiff brush to remove any grit or weed. Pull out the beards. Discard any open mussels that don't close when tapped on the benchtop.
2 Heat the oil in a large, deep, lidded frying pan, add the black beans, garlic, ginger, chilli and coriander root, and cook over low heat for 2–3 minutes, or until fragrant.
3 Add the wine and increase the heat to high. Add half the mussels in a single layer and cover with a tight-fitting lid. Cook for 2–3 minutes, or until the mussels have just opened. Discard any that do not open. Remove from the pan, and repeat with the remaining mussels.
4 Transfer the mussels to a serving dish, leaving the cooking liquid in the pan. Add the lime juice, sugar and coriander leaves to the pan and cook for 30 seconds. Pour the sauce over the mussels and serve immediately with rice.

Nutrition per serve: Fat 8 g; Protein 22 g; Carbohydrate 14 g; Dietary Fibre 1 g; Cholesterol 73.5 mg; 970 kJ (230 Cal)

Vietnamese duck rice paper rolls (top), and Mussels with black beans and coriander

THAI BEEF SKEWERS WITH PEANUT SAUCE

Ready to eat in 30 minutes
Serves 4

1 onion, chopped
2 cloves garlic, crushed
2 teaspoons sambal oelek
1 stem lemon grass, white part only, chopped
2 teaspoons chopped fresh ginger
1 1/2 tablespoons oil
270 ml coconut cream
1/2 cup (125 g) crunchy peanut butter
1 1/2 tablespoons fish sauce
2 teaspoons soy sauce
1 tablespoon grated palm sugar or soft brown sugar
2 tablespoons lime juice
2 tablespoons chopped fresh coriander leaves
750 g round or rump steak, cut into 2 cm x 10 cm pieces
2 teaspoons oil
fresh red chilli, chopped, to garnish (optional)
chopped roasted peanuts, to garnish (optional)

1 Put the onion, garlic, sambal oelek, lemon grass and ginger in a food processor and process to a smooth paste.
2 Heat the oil in a saucepan over medium heat, add the paste and cook, stirring, for 2–3 minutes, or until fragrant. Add the coconut cream, peanut butter, fish sauce, soy sauce, sugar and lime juice and bring to the boil. Reduce the heat and simmer for 5 minutes, then stir in the coriander.
3 Meanwhile, thread the meat onto 12 metal skewers, and cook on a hot chargrill or in a non-stick frying pan with the oil for 2 minutes each side, or until cooked to your liking. Serve the skewers on a bed of rice with the sauce and a salad on the side. Garnish with chopped chilli and peanuts, if desired.

Nutrition per serve: Fat 48.5 g; Protein 53 g; Carbohydrate 13 g; Dietary Fibre 6 g; Cholesterol 120 mg; 2910 kJ (695 Cal)

Note: If using wooden skewers, soak them for 30 minutes before grilling to prevent them from burning.

SWEET CHILLI AND GINGER SWORDFISH

Ready to eat in 20 minutes
Serves 4

4 swordfish steaks
1/4 cup (60 ml) peanut oil
3 cloves garlic, finely chopped
2 tablespoons grated fresh ginger
1/4 cup (60 ml) lime juice
1/3 cup (80 ml) sweet chilli sauce

1 Place the swordfish steaks in a non-metallic bowl, brush lightly with a little of the oil and top each steak with some combined garlic and ginger.
2 Heat the remaining oil in a non-stick frying pan. Add the swordfish with the topping facing up. Cook over medium heat for 2 minutes, or until crisp and golden on the underside.
3 Combine 1 tablespoon each of the lime juice and sweet chilli sauce and drizzle over the steaks. Carefully turn over and cook for 2 minutes, or until tender but still pink in the middle. Remove and keep warm.
4 Add the remaining lime juice and sweet chilli sauce, bring to the boil and cook for 1 minute, or until the sauce is thickened. Serve with steamed lemon grass and lime rice (page 32) and stir-fried vegetables.

Nutrition per serve: Fat 17.5 g; Protein 33 g; Carbohydrate 4 g; Dietary Fibre 1 g; Cholesterol 93 mg; 1275 kJ (305 Cal)

Thai beef skewers with peanut sauce (top), and Sweet chilli and ginger swordfish

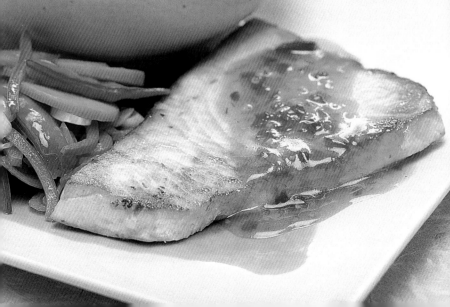

SALT AND PEPPER SQUID

Ready to eat in 20 minutes
Serves 4

1 cup (125 g) cornflour
1 1/2 tablespoons salt
1 tablespoon ground white pepper
3 small fresh red chillies, seeded, chopped
1 kg cleaned squid tubes, sliced into rings
2 egg whites, lightly beaten
oil, for deep-frying
lime wedges, for serving

1 Combine the cornflour, salt, pepper and chilli in a bowl.
2 Dip the squid rings into the beaten egg white and then into the cornflour mixture. Shake off any excess cornflour.
3 Fill a deep, heavy-based saucepan one third full of oil and heat to 180°C (350°F), or until a cube of bread dropped into the oil browns in 15 seconds. Cook the squid in batches for 1–2 minutes, or until lightly golden all over. Drain on crumpled paper towels. Serve hot with steamed rice and lime wedges.

Nutrition per serve: Fat 5.5 g; Protein 40 g; Carbohydrate 27 g; Dietary Fibre 0.5 g; Cholesterol 448 mg; 1330 kJ (320 Cal)

Salt and pepper squid (top), and Prawn rice noodle rolls

PRAWN RICE NOODLE ROLLS

Ready to eat in 30 minutes
Serves 4

1 tablespoon peanut oil
2 cloves garlic, crushed
200 g fresh shiitake mushrooms, thinly sliced
5 spring onions, chopped
1/3 cup (60 g) drained and chopped water chestnuts
150 g fresh baby corn, roughly chopped
650 g raw medium prawns, peeled, deveined and roughly chopped (see Note)
500 g fresh rice noodle rolls
oil, for brushing

Sauce
1/4 cup (60 ml) light soy sauce
2 teaspoons sesame oil
1 teaspoon grated fresh ginger
1 teaspoon sugar
2 tablespoons Chinese rice wine

1 Heat a wok over high heat, add the oil and swirl to coat. Add the garlic and mushrooms and stir-fry for 1 minute, or until soft. Then add the spring onion, water chestnuts, baby corn and prawns. Cook for 2 minutes, or until the corn is just tender and the prawns are beginning to turn pink, then remove from the heat.
2 Carefully unroll the rice noodle roll and cut it in half. You need two 24 cm x 16 cm rectangles. Place 1/4 cup of the prawn mixture along one short end of each rectangle, leaving a 3 cm border. Fold both sides of the noodle roll towards the centre, then roll up like a spring roll. Cover with a damp tea towel and repeat with the remaining noodle rolls and prawn mixture.
3 Line a bamboo steamer with baking paper, brush with a little oil, then place the rolls in, seam-side-down. Place the steamer over a wok filled with simmering water, and steam for 4–5 minutes, or until the prawns are cooked through.
4 Meanwhile, place the soy sauce, sesame oil, ginger, sugar and rice wine in a small saucepan and stir over medium heat to warm through. Place the rolls on a platter and drizzle with the sauce just before serving.

Nutrition per serve: Fat 8.5 g; Protein 31 g; Carbohydrate 44 g; Dietary Fibre 3.5 g; Cholesterol 186 mg; 1625 kJ (390 Cal)

Note: If you can't buy peeled raw prawns, buy 1.3 kg and peel them yourself. This will add about 15 minutes to your preparation time.

FLAVOURED RICE

One cup (200 g) raw rice makes 3 cups (550 g) cooked rice. Allow 1¹/2–2 cups of cooked rice per person. To cook rice for four by the absorption method, put 2¹/2 cups (500 g) rice in a sieve and wash under cold water until the water runs clear, then place in a large saucepan with 3 cups (750 ml) water, bring to the boil and boil for 1 minute. Cover with a tight-fitting lid, then reduce the heat as low as possible and cook for 10 minutes. Turn off the heat, cover and sit for 10 minutes. Fluff the rice with a fork.

COCONUT AND GINGER RICE

Wash 2 cups (400 g) long-grain rice and place in a saucepan with 2¹/2 cups (625 ml) water, ³/4 cup (45 g) shredded coconut, 2 teaspoons finely grated fresh ginger and 1 teaspoon salt. Stir to combine and bring to the boil over high heat. Reduce the heat to very low, stir and cover with a tight-fitting lid. Cook for 5–6 minutes, then turn off the heat and leave for 10 minutes. Fluff the rice with a fork. Serve immediately. Serves 6.

LEMON GRASS AND LIME RICE

Wash 2 cups (400 g) long-grain rice. Place in a saucepan with 1 cup (250 ml) water, 2 cups (500 ml) coconut cream, 1 bruised lemon grass stem, white part only, 2 kaffir lime leaves and 1 teaspoon salt. Bring to the boil over high heat, stir and reduce the heat to very low. Cover with a tight-fitting lid and cook for 15 minutes. Remove from the heat and leave to stand, covered, for 5 minutes. Lightly stir the rice with a fork to incorporate any coconut cream which has not been absorbed. Remove the lemon grass and lime leaves. Serves 4–6.

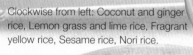

Clockwise from left: Coconut and ginger rice, Lemon grass and lime rice, Fragrant yellow rice, Sesame rice, Nori rice.

Fragrant yellow rice

Heat 20 g ghee in a frying pan, add 3 sliced red Asian shallots and cook for 5 minutes. Add 6 curry leaves and cook for a further 4 minutes, or until the shallots are golden. Add 1 teaspoon ground turmeric and 1 teaspoon salt, and cook for 1 minute. Fork the spice mixture through 6 cups (1.1 kg) cooked, warm rice. Serves 4.

Sesame rice

Wash 2 1/2 cups (500 g) long-grain rice and place in a saucepan with 3 cups (750 ml) water and 1 teaspoon salt. Bring to the boil over medium heat, cover with a tight-fitting lid, turn the heat down to very low and cook for 15 minutes. Remove from the heat and leave to stand for another 5 minutes without stirring or lifting the lid. Meanwhile, heat 2 teaspoons sesame oil in a small saucepan and cook 2 tablespoons white sesame seeds over low heat until golden brown. Add 1 tablespoon black sesame seeds and 1 tablespoon lime juice. Lightly fluff the rice with a fork and stir in the dressing. Serves 4.

Nori rice

Wash 2 cups (400 g) medium-grain rice until the water runs clear, then place in a saucepan with 2 1/2 cups (625 ml) water. Bring to the boil, then cover with a tight-fitting lid, turn the heat down to very low and cook for 15 minutes. Mix 3 1/2 tablespoons rice wine vinegar, 2 tablespoons mirin, 2 teaspoons sugar and 1/2 teaspoon salt in a small bowl. Pour over the rice and fluff with a fork to separate the grains. Fold in 1 sheet finely shredded nori and 1 tablespoon chopped pickled ginger. Serves 4.

CHILLI LAMB CUTLETS

Ready to eat in 30 minutes
Serves 4–6

4 cloves garlic, crushed
1 tablespoon grated fresh
  ginger
1 teaspoon oil
1 teaspoon sambal oelek
2 teaspoons ground
  coriander
2 teaspoons ground cumin
2 tablespoons soy sauce
2 teaspoons sesame oil
2 tablespoons sweet chilli
  sauce
2 tablespoons lemon juice
12 lamb cutlets

1 Combine the garlic, ginger, oil, sambal oelek, ground coriander, ground cumin, soy sauce, sesame oil, sweet chilli sauce and lemon juice in a bowl. Season with salt and cracked black pepper. Place the cutlets in a non-metallic dish and pour on the marinade, coating all sides. Leave to marinate for 20 minutes.
2 Cook the cutlets on a very hot chargrill plate or barbecue for 3 minutes each side, or until cooked to your liking. Serve the cutlets with lemon grass and lime rice or coconut and ginger rice (page 32).

Nutrition per serve (6): Fat 13.5 g;
Protein 19 g; Carbohydrate 4 g;
Dietary Fibre 1.5 g; Cholesterol
64 mg; 890 kJ (210 Cal)

FAMILY BEEF STIR-FRY

Ready to eat in 30 minutes
Serves 4

2 tablespoons peanut oil
350 g beef fillet, partially
  frozen, thinly sliced
  (see Note)
1 large onion, cut into thin
  wedges
1 large carrot, thinly sliced
  on the diagonal
1 red capsicum, cut into thin
  strips
100 g snow peas, sliced in
  half diagonally
150 g baby corn, sliced in
  half diagonally
200 g straw mushrooms,
  drained
2 tablespoons oyster sauce
1 clove garlic, crushed
1 teaspoon grated fresh
  ginger
2 tablespoons light soy
  sauce
2 tablespoons medium
  sherry
1 tablespoon honey
1 teaspoon sesame oil
2 teaspoons cornflour

1 Heat a wok over high heat, add 1 tablespoon of the peanut oil and swirl around to coat the side of the wok. Add the meat in batches and cook for 2–3 minutes, or until nicely browned. Remove the meat from the wok and keep warm.
2 Heat the remaining peanut oil in the wok, add the onion, carrot and capsicum and cook, stirring, for 2–3 minutes, or until the vegetables are just tender. Add the snow peas, corn and straw mushrooms, cook for a further minute, then return all the meat to the wok.
3 Combine the oyster sauce with the garlic, ginger, soy sauce, sherry, honey, sesame oil and 1 tablespoon water in a small bowl, then add the mixture to the wok. Mix the cornflour with 1 tablespoon of water, add to the wok and cook for 1 minute, or until the sauce thickens. Season to taste with salt and freshly ground black pepper. Serve immediately with rice or thin egg noodles.

Nutrition per serve: Fat 16 g;
Protein 25 g; Carbohydrate 24 g;
Dietary Fibre 5 g; Cholesterol
59 mg; 1445 kJ (345 Cal)

Note: Stir-frying is a method of cooking food very quickly. For meat to cook as quickly as stir-fries demand, the meat needs to be cut up very thinly. Keeping the meat partially frozen makes this much easier as the knife cuts through the meat much more smoothly than if the meat was at room temperature.

Chilli lamb cutlets (top),
and Family beef stir-fry

JAPANESE WARM CHICKEN SALAD

Ready to eat in 30 minutes
Serves 4

1 tablespoon grated fresh
   ginger
1/2 cup (125 ml) Japanese
   soy sauce
1/4 cup (60 ml) mirin
1 teaspoon chilli oil
1/2 cup (60 g) cornflour
750 g chicken breast fillets,
   cut into 3 cm cubes
1 teaspoon wasabi paste
1/2 cup (125 g) Japanese
   mayonnaise (see Note)
2 tablespoons oil
2 cups (80 g) mizuna,
   washed and picked over
1/2 avocado, sliced into thin
   wedges
2 tablespoons pickled
   ginger, shredded

1 Combine the ginger,
soy sauce, mirin, chilli
oil and cornflour in a
bowl, add the chicken
and toss to coat. In a
separate small bowl, mix
together the wasabi and
mayonnaise.
2 Heat a wok over high
heat. Add half the oil
and swirl it around to
coat the side of the wok.
Add half the chicken and
stir-fry for 4–5 minutes,
or until it is browned
and cooked through.
Remove the chicken
from the wok and keep
warm. Repeat with the

remaining oil and
chicken.
3 Divide the mizuna
and avocado among four
serving plates, top each
plate with an even
amount of the chicken,
and serve with the
mayonnaise and pickled
ginger.

Nutrition per serve: Fat 26 g;
Protein 43 g; Carbohydrate 19 g;
Dietary Fibre 1.5 g; Cholesterol
131.5 mg; 2030 kJ (485 Cal)

Note: Japanese mayonnaise is
available in Asian grocery stores.
It usually comes in an easy-to-
use squeeze bottle. If you can't
find Japanese mayonnaise, use
whole-egg mayonnaise instead.

SUKIYAKI SOUP

Ready to eat in 30 minutes
Serves 4–6

10 g dried sliced shiitake
   mushrooms
100 g dried rice vermicelli
2 teaspoons oil
1 leek, halved and sliced
1 litre chicken stock
1 teaspoon dashi granules
   dissolved in 2 cups
   (500 ml) boiling water
1/2 cup (125 ml) soy sauce
2 tablespoons mirin
1 1/2 tablespoons sugar
2 cups (100 g) shredded
   Chinese cabbage
   (wom buk)
300 g silken firm tofu, cut
   into 2 cm cubes
600 g rump steak, thinly
   sliced
4 spring onions, sliced
   diagonally

1 Soak the shiitake
mushrooms in 1/2 cup
(125 ml) boiling water
for 10 minutes. Place
the noodles in a large
heatproof bowl, cover
with boiling water and
leave them to stand for
5 minutes, then drain.
2 Heat the oil in a large
saucepan, add the leek
and cook over medium
heat for 3 minutes, or
until softened. Add the
chicken stock, dashi
broth, soy sauce, mirin,
sugar and mushrooms
and their soaking liquid.
Bring to the boil, then
reduce the heat and
simmer for 5 minutes.
3 Add the cabbage
and simmer for a further
5 minutes. Next, add
the tofu and beef, and
simmer for 5 minutes,
or until the beef is
cooked but still tender.
Divide the noodles
among the serving bowls
and ladle on the soup.
Serve garnished with the
spring onion.

Nutrition per serve (6): Fat 12 g;
Protein 37 g; Carbohydrate 27 g;
Dietary Fibre 2 g; Cholesterol
77 mg; 1530 kJ (365 Cal)

Japanese warm
chicken salad (top),
and Sukiyaki soup

BAKED FISH WITH COCONUT AND KAFFIR LIME

Ready to eat in 30 minutes
Serves 4

2 stems lemon grass, white
  part only
8 kaffir lime leaves
1 cup (250 ml) thick coconut
  cream
2 tablespoons fish sauce
1/2 teaspoon garam masala
2 teaspoons grated fresh
  ginger
2 cloves garlic, crushed
2 tablespoons chopped
  fresh coriander
4 x 200 g blue eye fillets
2 cm x 2 cm piece galangal,
  sliced into 4 pieces
1 lime, cut into wedges

1 Preheat the oven to moderately hot 200°C (400°F/Gas 6). Finely chop one lemon grass stem. Quarter the other lengthways and bruise it with the back of a knife.
2 Finely shred four of the lime leaves and place in a bowl with the coconut cream, fish sauce, garam masala, ginger, garlic, coriander, and finely chopped lemon grass. Mix together thoroughly, add the fish and toss to coat well.
3 Place a piece of bruised lemon grass and a piece of galangal in the centre of four 30 cm long pieces of baking paper. Place a fish fillet on top, place 1 kaffir lime leaf on top of each fillet and spoon on 1/4 cup of the coconut mixture. Wrap up securely and then wrap each parcel in foil.
4 Place in a non-metallic baking dish and bake for 15–20 minutes, or until cooked through. Unwrap the fish, discard the lemon grass and galangal pieces and serve on rice with the remaining cooking juices. Garnish with the lime wedges.

Nutrition per serve: Fat 17.5 g; Protein 43 g; Carbohydrate 3.5 g; Dietary Fibre 1.5 g; Cholesterol 118 mg; 1430 kJ (340 Cal)

RED CURRY OF ROAST PUMPKIN, BEANS AND BASIL

Ready to eat in 30 minutes
Serves 4

600 g peeled and seeded
  pumpkin, cut into
  3 cm cubes
2 tablespoons oil
1 tablespoon ready-made
  red curry paste
400 ml coconut cream
  (see Note)
200 g green beans, cut into
  3 cm lengths
2 kaffir lime leaves, crushed
1 tablespoon grated light
  palm sugar
1 tablespoon fish sauce
1 cup (30 g) fresh Thai basil
  leaves, plus extra to
  garnish
1 tablespoon lime juice

1 Preheat the oven to moderately hot 200°C (400°F/Gas 6). Place the pumpkin in a baking dish with 1 tablespoon oil and toss to coat. Bake for 20 minutes, or until tender.
2 Heat the remaining oil in a saucepan, add the curry paste and cook, stirring constantly, breaking up with a fork, over medium heat for 1–2 minutes. Add the coconut cream 1/2 cup (125 ml) at a time, stirring well with a wooden spoon between each addition for a creamy consistency. Then add the pumpkin and any roasting juices, the beans and kaffir lime leaves. Reduce the heat to low and cook for 5 minutes.
3 Stir in the palm sugar, fish sauce, basil and lime juice. Garnish with extra fresh basil leaves. Serve with rice.

Nutrition per serve: Fat 32.5 g; Protein 7 g; Carbohydrate 18.5 g; Dietary Fibre 6 g; Cholesterol 0.05 mg; 1630 kJ (390 Cal)

Note: If you want to make this a less fattening meal, substitute the coconut cream for the lite version; the texture will be slightly different but the flavour of the curry will still be good.

Baked fish with coconut and kaffir lime (top), and Red curry of roast pumpkin, beans and basil

BEEF AND GLASS NOODLE SALAD
Ready to eat in 30 minutes
Serves 4

250 g mung bean thread
    vermicelli (glass noodles)
2 teaspoons oil
400 g fillet steak
1 small fresh red chilli, finely
    chopped
6 spring onions, finely sliced
1/4 cup (60 ml) lime juice
1/4 cup (60 ml) fish sauce
2 teaspoons grated light
    palm sugar
1 small red capsicum, very
    thinly sliced
1/2 red onion, thinly sliced
1 cup (20 g) fresh mint
1 cup (30 g) fresh Thai basil

1 Place the noodles in
a heatproof bowl, cover
with boiling water and
leave for 5 minutes.
Drain, rinse in cold
water and drain well.
Chop into 10 cm lengths
with scissors.
2 Heat the oil in a
frying pan, add the steak
and cook for 2 minutes
each side, or until
medium–rare. Remove,
cover and leave to rest
for 5 minutes.
3 Place the chilli, spring
onion, lime juice, fish
sauce and sugar in a
small bowl, and mix
together well.
4 Thinly slice the beef
and place in a large bowl

Beef and glass noodle salad
(top), and Chinese-style
'drunken' chicken

with the noodles,
capsicum, red onion,
mint and Thai basil. Add
the dressing, toss to coat
and serve.

Nutrition per serve: Fat 7.5 g;
Protein 24 g; Carbohydrate 59 g;
Dietary Fibre 2 g; Cholesterol
67 mg; 1675 kJ (400 Cal)

CHINESE-STYLE 'DRUNKEN' CHICKEN
Ready to eat in 30 minutes
Serves 4

1 kg chicken breast fillets,
    cut into 2.5 cm cubes
2 egg whites
1/4 cup (60 ml) Chinese rice
    wine
2 tablespoons cornflour
8–10 spring onions, thinly
    sliced
1 cup (50 g) chopped fresh
    coriander leaves
3 teaspoons finely chopped
    fresh ginger
1 large clove garlic, finely
    chopped
1/3 cup (80 ml) peanut oil
1/4 cup (60 ml) light soy
    sauce
1 teaspoon sesame oil

1 Place the chicken in a
large bowl. Place the egg
whites, 2 tablespoons
rice wine, cornflour and
1 teaspoon salt in a food
processor and process for
30 seconds, or until the
mixture is smooth and
thick. Pour over the
chicken and toss to coat.
Leave for 10 minutes.

2 Fill a large saucepan
three-quarters full of
water and bring to the
boil. Gently place the
chicken in the boiling
water and stir to
separate. Turn the heat
off, cover and leave
for 5 minutes, or until
cooked through. Drain
well and leave to rest
for 5 minutes.
3 Place the spring
onion, coriander, ginger
and garlic in a heatproof
bowl, and mix together
well. Heat the oil in
a small saucepan over
high heat until very
hot. When the oil is
smoking, pour it over
the spring onion mixture
and toss for 30 seconds.
Add the soy sauce,
remaining rice wine and
sesame oil, and stir to
combine.
4 Place the chicken on a
serving platter with the
sauce spooned over the
top. Serve with rice.

Nutrition per serve: Fat 33.5 g;
Protein 57 g; Carbohydrate 7 g;
Dietary Fibre 0.5 g; Cholesterol
165 mg; 2375 kJ (565 Cal)

STIR-FRIED LAMB WITH MINT AND CHILLI
Ready to eat in 20 minutes
Serves 4

1 tablespoon oil
750 g lamb fillet, thinly
  sliced (see Note)
4 cloves garlic, finely
  chopped
2 small fresh red chillies,
  thinly sliced
1/3 cup (80 ml) oyster sauce
2 1/2 tablespoons fish sauce
1 1/2 teaspoons sugar
1/2 cup (25 g) chopped
  fresh mint
1/4 cup (5 g) whole fresh
  mint leaves

1 Heat a wok over high heat, add the oil and swirl to coat. Add the lamb and garlic in batches and stir-fry for 1–2 minutes, or until the lamb is almost cooked. Return all the lamb to the wok. Stir in the chilli, oyster sauce, fish sauce, sugar and the chopped mint leaves, and cook for another 1–2 minutes.
2 Remove from the heat, fold in the whole mint leaves and serve immediately with rice.

Nutrition per serve: Fat 23.5 g; Protein 44 g; Carbohydrate 8 g; Dietary Fibre 1.5 g; Cholesterol 133 mg; 1745 kJ (415 Cal)

Note: Make sure you slice the lamb across the grain—this will minimise the meat breaking up and shrinking when cooking.

YELLOW FISH CURRY
Ready to eat in 25 minutes
Serves 4

150 ml vegetable stock
1 tablespoon ready-made
  yellow curry paste (see
  Note)
1 tablespoon tamarind
  purée
1 tablespoon grated palm
  sugar or soft brown sugar
1 1/2 tablespoons fish sauce
150 g green beans, trimmed
  and cut into 4 cm lengths
1 cup (140 g) sliced, canned
  bamboo shoots, rinsed
  and drained
400 ml coconut cream
400 g perch fillet, cubed
1 tablespoon lime juice
lime wedges, to serve
fresh coriander leaves,
  to garnish

1 Place the stock in a large saucepan and bring to the boil. Add the curry paste and cook, stirring, for 3–4 minutes, or until fragrant. Stir in the combined tamarind purée, palm sugar and 1 tablespoon of the fish sauce. Add the beans and bamboo shoots, and cook over medium heat for 3–5 minutes, or until the beans are almost tender.
2 Add the coconut cream and bring to the boil, then reduce the heat, add the fish and simmer for 3–5 minutes, or until the fish is just cooked. Stir in the lime juice and remaining fish sauce. Garnish with the lime wedges and fresh coriander leaves. Serve with rice.

Nutrition per serve: Fat 22 g; Protein 21 g; Carbohydrate 9.5 g; Dietary Fibre 4 g; Cholesterol 20 mg; 1335 kJ (320 Cal)

Note: Ready-made yellow curry paste can be bought at supermarkets and Asian food stores, but if time permits, try making your own—it is very easy and will only take about 20 minutes. Place 8 small green chillies, 5 roughly chopped red Asian shallots, 2 cloves chopped garlic, 1 tablespoon finely chopped coriander stem and root, 1 chopped stem of lemon grass (white part only), 2 tablespoons finely chopped fresh galangal, 1 teaspoon ground coriander, 1 teaspoon ground cumin, 1/2 teaspoon ground turmeric, 1/2 teaspoon black peppercorns and 1 tablespoon lime juice in a food processor, blender or mortar and pestle. Process or grind into a smooth paste. Store in an airtight container in the refrigerator for up to a month. Makes 1/2 cup.

Stir-fried lamb
with mint and chilli (top)
and Yellow fish curry

BRAISED WATER SPINACH WITH TOFU
Ready to eat in 20 minutes
Serves 4

500 g firm tofu (see Hint)
1/4 cup (60 ml) oil
1 clove garlic, chopped
2 cm x 2 cm piece fresh ginger, chopped
750 g water spinach, cut into 4 cm lengths
2 tablespoons kecap manis
2 tablespoons soy sauce
1 tablespoon toasted sesame seeds

1 Drain the tofu on paper towels and cut into 2 cm cubes. Heat a wok or large frying pan over high heat, add 2 tablespoons of the oil and swirl to coat the surface of the wok. Add the tofu and cook, turning occasionally, for 5 minutes, or until lightly browned. Drain on crumpled paper towels.
2 Heat the remaining oil in the wok, add the garlic and ginger and stir-fry for 1 minute. Stir in the water spinach, kecap manis, soy sauce and 1 tablespoon water, toss well, then add the tofu and gently stir for 1 minute, or until the water spinach has wilted.

Braised water spinach with tofu (top), and Chinese omelettes with mushroom sauce

Serve immediately, sprinkled with the sesame seeds. Serve with rice.

Nutrition per serve: Fat 24.5 g; Protein 22 g; Carbohydrate 4 g; Dietary Fibre 8 g; Cholesterol 0 mg; 1335 kJ (320 Cal)

Hint: To reduce cooking time you can use pre-fried tofu if available.

Variation: Any leafy Asian green or English spinach can replace the water spinach.

CHINESE OMELETTES WITH MUSHROOM SAUCE
Ready to eat in 30 minutes
Serves 2–4

6 whole dried Chinese mushrooms
6 eggs, lightly beaten
4 spring onions, thinly sliced
1 small red capsicum, thinly sliced
1 cup (90 g) bean sprouts
2 teaspoons sesame oil
1 teaspoon soy sauce
1 tablespoon oil
1 1/2 tablespoons oil, extra
2 cloves garlic, crushed
1 cup (250 ml) chicken stock
1 tablespoon oyster sauce
2 teaspoons soy sauce
1 teaspoon sugar
2 spring onions, sliced diagonally, extra
2 teaspoons cornflour

1 Place the mushrooms in a heatproof bowl, cover with boiling water and leave to soak for 15 minutes. Drain, discard the stems and thinly slice the caps.

2 Meanwhile, place the egg, spring onion, capsicum, bean sprouts, sesame oil and soy sauce in a bowl and mix together well. Season.
3 Heat a wok or frying pan over high heat, add 2 teaspoons oil and swirl to coat. Place a quarter of the egg mixture in the wok, swirl to coat evenly and cook for 1–2 minutes, or until the egg is almost set. Turn over and cook the other side for 1 minute, or until brown. Remove and keep warm. Repeat with the remaining mixture, adding more oil if necessary.
4 Reheat the wok or frying pan over high heat, add the extra oil and swirl to coat. Add the garlic and mushrooms and cook for 1 minute, or until the garlic is fragrant. Add the stock, oyster sauce, soy sauce, sugar and extra spring onion. Bring to the boil, then reduce the heat and simmer for 1 minute. Combine the cornflour with 1 tablespoon water, add to the wok and simmer for 2 minutes, or until thickened slightly. Serve the omelettes topped with the sauce.

Nutrition per serve (4): Fat 22 g; Protein 12 g; Carbohydrate 8 g; Dietary Fibre 1.5 g; Cholesterol 281 mg; 1130 kJ (270 Cal)

STIR-FRIED SCALLOPS WITH SUGAR SNAP PEAS

Ready to eat in 25 minutes
Serves 4

2 tablespoons oil
2 large cloves garlic, crushed
3 teaspoons finely chopped fresh ginger
300 g sugar snap peas
500 g scallops without roe, membrane removed
2 spring onions, cut into 2 cm lengths
2 1/2 tablespoons oyster sauce
2 teaspoons soy sauce
1/2 teaspoon sesame oil
2 teaspoons sugar

1 Heat a wok or frying pan over medium heat, add the oil and swirl to coat the surface of the wok. Add the garlic and ginger and stir-fry for 30 seconds, or until fragrant.
2 Add the peas to the wok and cook for 1 minute, then add the scallops and spring onion and cook for 1 minute, or until the spring onion is wilted. Stir in the oyster and soy sauces, sesame oil and sugar and heat for 1 minute, or until heated through and combined. Serve with rice.

Nutrition per serve: Fat 11 g; Protein 18 g; Carbohydrate 10 g; Dietary Fibre 2 g; Cholesterol 41.5 mg; 875 kJ (210 Cal)

JAPANESE CHICKEN LOAF WITH SALAD

Ready to eat in 20 minutes
Serves 4

500 g chicken breast fillets, roughly chopped
2 large spring onions, thinly sliced
2 teaspoons soy sauce
1 teaspoon caster sugar
2 teaspoons sake or dry white wine
1 1/2 teaspoons grated fresh ginger
1 egg, lightly beaten
2 teaspoons peanut oil
1 tablespoon toasted sesame seeds

Salad
2 teaspoons oil
2 teaspoons sesame oil
1 1/2 tablespoons soy sauce
1 tablespoon rice wine vinegar
250 g watercress
250 g cherry tomatoes, halved
1 cucumber, seeded, julienned

1 Place the chicken, spring onion, soy sauce, sugar, sake, ginger and 1 1/2 tablespoons beaten egg in a food processor, and process until combined. Season with salt and freshly ground black pepper.
2 Heat the oil in a 20 cm heavy-based stainless steel frying pan and add the chicken mixture. Using a wet spatula, quickly spread the chicken evenly to form a 1 cm thick cake. Cook over medium heat for 3 minutes, or until the base is golden brown.
3 Cut the cake into four wedges and turn each wedge over. Sprinkle with the sesame seeds and cook for 2 minutes, or until the chicken is cooked.
4 To make the salad, place the oil, sesame oil, soy sauce and vinegar in a small bowl, and mix together well. Place the watercress, tomatoes and cucumber in a large bowl, pour on the dressing and toss well. Serve the chicken loaf immediately with the salad.

Nutrition per serve: Fat 12 g; Protein 30 g; Carbohydrate 2 g; Dietary Fibre 0.5 g; Cholesterol 129.5 mg; 990 kJ (235 Cal)

Note: This dish is best prepared in a regular stainless steel (not non-stick) frying pan, otherwise it tends to steam and doesn't brown well.

Stir-fried scallops with sugar snap peas (top), and Japanese chicken loaf with salad

ROAST DUCK AND NOODLE SALAD
Ready to eat in 30 minutes
Serves 4

400 g fresh flat Chinese egg
  noodles
1 teaspoon sesame oil, plus
  1 tablespoon extra
1 tablespoon grated fresh
  ginger
1/2–1 teaspoon sambal
  oelek, or to taste
2 tablespoons fish sauce
2 tablespoons rice wine
  vinegar
1 tablespoon lime juice
1/4 teaspoon Chinese
  five-spice powder
1 tablespoon soft brown
  sugar
2 tablespoons peanut oil
1 cup (50 g) roughly
  chopped fresh coriander,
  plus extra leaves,
  to garnish
1 Chinese roast duck, meat
  removed from bones and
  sliced into bite-size pieces
2 cups (180 g) bean sprouts
3 spring onions, thinly sliced
1/2 cup (80 g) roasted
  peanuts, chopped

1 Bring a large saucepan
of lightly salted water
to the boil. Add the
noodles and cook for
3–4 minutes, or until
just tender. Rinse under
cold water, drain and
toss with 1 teaspoon
sesame oil.
2 Place the ginger,
sambal oelek, fish sauce,
vinegar, lime juice,
five-spice and sugar in
a small bowl and stir
to dissolve the sugar.
Whisk in the extra
sesame oil and the
peanut oil, then stir in
the coriander. Season
to taste with salt.
3 Place the noodles,
duck, bean sprouts and
spring onion in a large
bowl. Pour on the
dressing and toss to coat.
Season to taste. Garnish
with the chopped
peanuts and extra
coriander leaves.

Nutrition per serve: Fat 35 g;
Protein 41 g; Carbohydrate 82 g;
Dietary Fibre 6.5 g; Cholesterol
131.5 mg; 3360 kJ (805 Cal)

CHINESE BEEF AND BROCCOLI STIR-FRY
Ready to eat in 25 minutes
Serves 4

1/4 cup (60 ml) peanut oil
1 kg fresh rice noodle rolls,
  cut into 2 cm strips,
  separated
500 g rump steak, trimmed
  and thinly sliced
1 onion, cut into wedges
4 cloves garlic, chopped
400 g Chinese broccoli,
  cut into 3 cm lengths
1 tablespoon soy sauce
1/4 cup (60 ml) kecap
  manis
1 small, fresh red chilli,
  chopped
1/2 cup (125 ml) beef stock

1 Heat a wok over
medium heat, add
2 tablespoons of the
peanut oil and swirl to
coat the side of the wok.
Add the noodles and
stir-fry gently for
2 minutes. Remove
from the wok.
2 Reheat the wok
over high heat, add the
remaining oil and swirl
to coat. Add the beef
in batches and cook
for 3 minutes, or until
browned. Remove
from the wok. Add the
onion and stir-fry for
1–2 minutes, then add
the garlic and cook for
a further 30 seconds.
3 Return all the beef
to the wok and add the
Chinese broccoli, soy
sauce, kecap manis,
chilli and beef stock, and
cook over medium heat
for 2–3 minutes. Divide
the noodles among four
serving plates and top
with the beef mixture.
Serve immediately.

Nutrition per serve: Fat 20.5 g;
Protein 36 g; Carbohydrate 54 g;
Dietary Fibre 4.5 g; Cholesterol
80 mg; 2285 kJ (545 Cal)

Note: The noodles may break
up during cooking. This will not
affect the flavour of the dish.

Roast duck and noodle
salad (top), and Chinese
beef and broccoli stir-fry

SPICY EGGPLANT STIR-FRY
Ready to eat in 30 minutes
Serves 4

1 tablespoon chilli bean sauce
2 tablespoons soy sauce
1 tablespoon rice wine vinegar
1/2 teaspoon sugar
1/4 cup (60 ml) oil
500 g eggplant, cubed
1 onion, cut into thin wedges
1 large fresh red chilli, seeded, sliced diagonally
2 cloves garlic, crushed
1/2 cup (15 g) fresh coriander leaves

1 Place the chilli bean sauce, soy sauce, rice wine vinegar and sugar in a small bowl, and whisk together well.
2 Heat a wok or frying pan over high heat, add 1 tablespoon of oil and swirl to coat. Add half the eggplant and cook, stirring, for 3–4 minutes, or until lightly browned. Drain on paper towels. Repeat with another tablespoon of oil and the remaining eggplant.
3 Reheat the wok over high heat, add the remaining oil and swirl to coat. Add the onion, chilli and garlic and cook over medium heat for 2 minutes. Return the eggplant to the wok, add the sauce and cook, covered, for 5 minutes. Remove from the heat and stir in the coriander leaves. Serve with rice.

Nutrition per serve: Fat 14.5 g; Protein 3 g; Carbohydrate 7.5 g; Dietary Fibre 4 g; Cholesterol 0.5 mg; 715 kJ (170 Cal)

Note: Chilli bean sauce is used in many Sichuan-style dishes. If unavailable, replace it with garlic chilli bean paste or sambal oelek, also available from selected supermarkets or Asian food stores.

FRIED NOODLES WITH CHICKEN, PORK AND PRAWN
Ready to eat in 30 minutes
Serves 4

900 g fresh flat rice noodle sheets, cut into 2 cm thick slices
100 ml oil
2 cloves garlic, finely chopped
1 tablespoon grated fresh ginger
70 g garlic chives, cut into 5 cm lengths
1/2 barbecue chicken, flesh cut into 1 cm slices
300 g Chinese barbecue pork fillet, cut into 1 cm slices
1 small fresh red chilli, chopped
12 large cooked prawns, peeled and deveined
2 cups (180 g) bean sprouts
100 g English spinach
2 eggs, beaten
2 teaspoons caster sugar
1/2 cup (125 ml) light soy sauce
2 tablespoons dark soy sauce
2 tablespoons fish sauce

1 Rinse the noodles under warm running water and carefully separate. Drain.
2 Heat a wok over high heat, add 1/4 cup (60 ml) of the oil and swirl to coat. Add the garlic and ginger, and cook, stirring, for 30 seconds. Be careful not to burn. Then add the chives and cook, stirring, for 10 seconds.
3 Add the chicken, pork, chilli and prawns, and cook, stirring, for 2 minutes, then add the bean sprouts and spinach, and cook, stirring, for 1 minute.
4 Make a well in the centre, add the egg and scramble for 1 minute, or until firm but not hard. Stir in the remaining oil, then add the rice noodles. Stir to combine. Add the combined sugar, soy sauces and fish sauce and stir-fry for 2–3 minutes, or until heated through. Season with pepper.

Nutrition per serve: Fat 38 g; Protein 54 g; Carbohydrate 54 g; Dietary Fibre 4 g; Cholesterol 286.5 mg; 3245 kJ (775 Cal)

Spicy eggplant stir-fry (top), and Fried noodles with chicken, pork and prawn

PORK, ASPARAGUS AND BABY CORN STIR-FRY
Ready to eat in 25 minutes
Serves 4

1 clove garlic, chopped
1 teaspoon grated fresh ginger
2 tablespoons soy sauce
1/4 teaspoon ground white pepper
1 tablespoon Chinese rice wine
600 g pork fillet, thinly sliced
1 tablespoon peanut oil
1 teaspoon sesame oil
6 fresh shiitake mushrooms, thinly sliced
150 g baby corn
100 g asparagus, cut into 4 cm lengths on the diagonal
2 tablespoons oyster sauce

1 Place the garlic, ginger, soy sauce, pepper and wine in a bowl and mix together well. Add all the pork and stir until it is well coated in the marinade.
2 Heat a wok over high heat, add half the oils and swirl to coat the side of the wok. Add half the pork mixture and stir-fry for about 2 minutes, or until the pork changes colour. Remove the pork from the wok. Repeat with the remaining oil and pork mixture.
3 Add the mushrooms, corn and asparagus to the wok and stir-fry for 2 minutes. Return the pork and any juices to the wok and stir in the oyster sauce. Cook, stirring, for another 2 minutes, or until it is evenly heated through. Divide among four plates and serve with rice.

Nutrition per serve: Fat 9.5 g; Protein 36 g; Carbohydrate 11 g; Dietary Fibre 2 g; Cholesterol 142.5 mg; 1180 kJ (280 Cal)

BRAISED VEGETABLES WITH CASHEWS
Ready to eat in 25 minutes
Serves 4

1 tablespoon peanut oil
2 cloves garlic, crushed
2 teaspoons grated fresh ginger
300 g choy sum, cut into 10 cm lengths
150 g baby corn, sliced in half on the diagonal
3/4 cup (185 ml) chicken or vegetable stock
200 g canned, drained bamboo shoots
150 g oyster mushrooms, sliced in half
2 teaspoons cornflour
2 tablespoons oyster sauce
2 teaspoons sesame oil
1 cup (90 g) bean sprouts
75 g roasted unsalted cashews

1 Heat a wok over medium heat, add the oil and swirl to coat. Add the garlic and ginger and stir-fry for 1 minute. Increase the heat to high, add the choy sum and baby corn and stir-fry for another minute.
2 Add the chicken stock and cook for 3–4 minutes, or until the choy sum stems are just tender. Add the bamboo shoots and mushrooms, and cook for 1 minute.
3 Place the cornflour and 1 tablespoon water in a small bowl and mix together well. Stir into the vegetables, along with the oyster sauce. Cook for 1–2 minutes, or until the sauce is slightly thickened. Stir in the sesame oil and bean sprouts and serve immediately on a bed of steamed rice sprinkled with the roasted cashews.

Nutrition per serve: Fat 18 g; Protein 13 g; Carbohydrate 65 g; Dietary Fibre 8 g; Cholesterol 0 mg; 1980 kJ (470 Cal)

Pork, asparagus and baby corn stir-fry (top), and Braised vegetables with cashews

CHICKEN BRAISED WITH GINGER AND STAR ANISE

Ready to eat in 30 minutes
Serves 4

1 teaspoon Sichuan
  peppercorns
2 tablespoons peanut oil
3 cm x 2 cm fresh ginger,
  julienned
2 cloves garlic, chopped
1 kg chicken thigh fillets,
  cut in half
1/3 cup (80 ml) Chinese rice
  wine
1 tablespoon honey
1/4 cup (60 ml) light soy
  sauce
1 star anise

1 Heat a wok over medium heat, add the peppercorns and cook, stirring to prevent burning, for 2–4 minutes, or until fragrant. Remove and lightly crush with the back of a knife.
2 Reheat the wok, add the oil and swirl to coat. Add the ginger and garlic, cook over low heat for 1–2 minutes, or until slightly golden. Add the chicken, increase the heat to medium and cook for 3 minutes, or until browned all over.
3 Add the peppercorns, wine, honey, soy sauce and star anise to the wok, reduce the heat to low and simmer, covered, for 20 minutes, or until the chicken is tender. Divide among four plates and serve with steamed rice.

Nutrition per serve: Fat 28 g; Protein 52 g; Carbohydrate 56 g; Dietary Fibre 1.5 g; Cholesterol 217.5 mg; 2940 kJ (705 Cal)

PORK WITH PLUM SAUCE AND CHOY SUM

Ready to eat in 30 minutes
Serves 4

600 g choy sum, cut into
  6 cm lengths
1/2 cup (125 ml) peanut oil
1 large onion, sliced
3 cloves garlic, finely
  chopped
2 teaspoons finely chopped
  fresh ginger
500 g pork loin, thinly sliced
2 tablespoons cornflour,
  seasoned with salt and
  pepper
1/4 cup (60 ml) plum sauce
1 1/2 tablespoons soy sauce
1 teaspoon sesame oil
2 tablespoons dry sherry or
  Chinese rice wine

1 Bring a large saucepan of lightly salted water to the boil, add the choy sum and cook for 2–3 minutes, or until the stems are crisp but still tender. Plunge into iced water to chill completely, then drain.
2 Heat a wok over high heat, add 1 tablespoon oil and swirl to coat. Add the onion, garlic and ginger and cook over medium heat for 3 minutes, or until softened. Remove from the wok.
3 Toss the pork in the seasoned cornflour to coat, shaking off any excess. Reheat the wok over high heat, add the remaining oil and swirl to coat. Add the pork in batches and cook for 3 minutes, or until golden on both sides. Remove.
4 Drain the oil from the wok and return the meat and any juices. Combine the plum sauce, soy sauce, sesame oil and sherry, and add to the wok. Cook over high heat for 2–3 minutes, then add the choy sum and return the onion mixture. Cook, stirring, for a further 2 minutes. Serve immediately with rice.

Nutrition per serve: Fat 33 g; Protein 30 g; Carbohydrate 18 g; Dietary Fibre 3 g; Cholesterol 118.5 mg; 2070 kJ (495 Cal)

Chicken braised with ginger and star anise (top), and Pork with plum sauce and choy sum

TUNA WITH CORIANDER CHUTNEY

Ready to eat in 15 minutes
Serves 4

45 g fresh coriander,
  including roots, roughly
  chopped
1/2 small white onion,
  roughly chopped
2 teaspoons grated fresh
  ginger
1/4 cup (25 g) desiccated
  coconut
2 teaspoons grated palm
  sugar or soft brown sugar
1 tablespoon lime juice
1 teaspoon fish sauce
1/4 cup (60 ml) oil
1 tablespoon olive oil
4 x 150 g tuna steaks

1 To make the
coriander chutney, place
the coriander, onion,
ginger, desiccated
coconut, sugar, lime
juice and fish sauce in a
food processor. Process
until smooth, then
gradually add the oil,
using the pulse button
until combined.
2 Heat the olive oil in a
frying pan, add the tuna
and cook over high heat
for 2–3 minutes each
side, or until cooked but
still pink in the middle.
Serve hot with lemon
grass and lime rice
(page 32) and a dollop
of the coriander
chutney.

Tuna with coriander chutney
(top) and Yakiudon

Nutrition per serve: Fat 31 g;
Protein 39 g; Carbohydrate 3.5 g;
Dietary Fibre 1.5 g; Cholesterol
54 mg; 1860 kJ (445 Cal)

YAKIUDON

Ready to eat in 30 minutes
Serves 4

5 dried shiitake mushrooms
1 clove garlic, crushed
2 teaspoons grated fresh
  ginger
1/2 cup (125 ml) Japanese
  soy sauce
2 tablespoons rice wine
  vinegar
2 tablespoons sugar
1 tablespoon lemon juice
500 g fresh Udon noodles
2 tablespoons oil
500 g chicken thigh fillets,
  thinly sliced
1 clove garlic, extra, finely
  chopped
1 small red capsicum, thinly
  sliced
2 cups (150 g) shredded
  cabbage
4 spring onions, thinly sliced
1 tablespoon sesame oil
white pepper, to taste
2 tablespoons drained
  shredded pickled ginger

1 Place the mushrooms
in a heatproof bowl and
cover with boiling water
for 10 minutes, or until
tender. Drain, reserving
1/4 cup (60 ml) soaking
liquid. Discard the
stems, squeeze dry the
caps and thinly slice.
2 Combine the crushed
garlic, ginger, Japanese
soy sauce, vinegar,
sugar, lemon juice and
reserved mushroom
soaking liquid in a jug.
3 Place the noodles in a
heatproof bowl, cover
with boiling water and
leave for 2 minutes, or
until soft and tender.
Drain.
4 Heat a wok over high
heat, add half the oil and
swirl to coat. Add the
chicken in batches and
stir-fry for 5 minutes,
or until browned.
Remove from the wok.
5 Add the remaining
oil and swirl to coat.
Add the extra garlic,
mushrooms, capsicum
and cabbage, and stir-fry
for 2–3 minutes, or until
softened. Add the
noodles and stir-fry for
a further 1 minute.
Return the chicken to
the wok and add the
spring onion, sesame oil
and soy sauce mixture,
stirring, until well
combined and heated
through. Season with
white pepper and scatter
with the pickled ginger.

Nutrition per serve: Fat 44.5 g;
Protein 38 g;Carbohydrate 81 g;
Dietary Fibre 12 g; Cholesterol
116 mg; 3665 kJ (875 Cal)

Note: This dish is also
commonly made using soba
noodles; in Japan it is then
called yakisoba.

CHILLI BEEF

Ready to eat in 30 minutes
Serves 4

1/4 cup (60 ml) kecap manis
21/2 teaspoons sambal oelek
2 cloves garlic, crushed
1/2 teaspoon ground
   coriander
1 tablespoon grated palm
   sugar or soft brown sugar
1 teaspoon sesame oil
400 g beef fillet, partially
   frozen, thinly sliced
1 tablespoon peanut oil
2 tablespoons chopped
   roasted peanuts
3 tablespoons chopped
   fresh coriander leaves

1 Combine the kecap manis, sambal oelek, garlic, ground coriander, palm sugar, sesame oil and 2 tablespoons water in a large bowl. Add the beef slices and coat well. Cover with plastic wrap and refrigerate for 20 minutes.
2 Heat a wok over high heat, add the peanut oil and swirl to coat. Add the meat in batches and cook each batch for 2–3 minutes, or until browned.
3 Arrange the beef on a serving platter, sprinkle with the chopped peanuts and fresh coriander, and serve with steamed rice.

Nutrition per serve: Fat 13.5 g;
Protein 24 g; Carbohydrate 5.5 g;
Dietary Fibre 1 g; Cholesterol
67 mg; 985 kJ (235 Cal)

KING PRAWNS WITH GARLIC SAUCE

Ready to eat in 30 minutes
Serves 4

500 g peeled, deveined, tails
   intact raw king prawns
   (see Note)
2 egg whites
2 tablespoons cornflour
2 tablespoons rice wine
   vinegar
oil, for deep-frying, plus
   1 tablespoon extra
125 g mung bean thread
   vermicelli, broken up into
   small pieces
4 cloves garlic, finely
   chopped
1 teaspoon finely chopped
   fresh ginger
2 teaspoons hoisin sauce
1 tablespoon bean sauce
1 tablespoon oyster sauce
6 spring onions, cut into
   3 cm pieces on the
   diagonal
1/2 cup (15 g) fresh
   coriander leaves
6 lemon wedges

1 Place the prawns in a large bowl. Process the egg white, cornflour and 1 tablespoon rice wine vinegar in a food processor until smooth. Pour over the prawns, season with 1 teaspoon salt and 1 teaspoon pepper, and stir to combine. Leave to stand for 10 minutes, then drain well.
2 Fill a large heavy-based saucepan one-third full of oil and heat to

190°C (375°F), or until a cube of bread dropped into the oil browns in 10 seconds. Add the noodles and cook for 10 seconds, or until puffed up. Drain on crumpled paper towels. Gently add the prawns to the pan, and cook for 2–3 minutes, or until the prawns change colour. Drain on crumpled paper towels.
3 Heat a wok over medium heat, add the extra oil and swirl to coat. Add the garlic and ginger and stir-fry for 30 seconds, then add the hoisin sauce, bean sauce, oyster sauce and the remaining vinegar, and stir to combine for 1 minute. Add the prawns to the sauce and toss to coat, then add the spring onion and cook for 1–2 minutes, or until soft. Arrange the prawns on a bed of crispy noodles, garnish with the coriander and serve with some lemon wedges on the side.

Nutrition per serve: Fat 10.5 g;
Protein 29 g; Carbohydrate 36 g;
Dietary Fibre 1.5 g; Cholesterol
186.5 mg; 1495 kJ (355 Cal)

Note: If peeled prawns are not available, buy 1 kg unpeeled prawns and peel them yourself. This will add about 15 minutes to your preparation.

Chilli beef (top), and King prawns with garlic sauce

CHICKEN TERIYAKI
Ready to eat in 30 minutes
Serves 4

1/3 cup (80 ml) dry sherry
1/3 cup (80 ml) soy sauce
1/3 cup (60 g) soft brown
  sugar
1 tablespoon finely chopped
  fresh ginger
2 small cloves garlic,
  crushed
500 g chicken breast fillets,
  cut into 3 cm cubes
oil, for brushing
1/4 cup (60 ml) peanut oil
10 spring onions, cut into
  3 cm lengths

1 Combine the sherry, soy sauce, sugar, ginger and garlic in a large shallow non-metallic dish and stir to dissolve the sugar. Add the chicken and toss to coat. Cover with plastic wrap and leave to stand for 10 minutes, tossing the chicken occasionally.
2 Brush a shallow baking tray with oil. Drain the chicken, reserving the marinade. Add the peanut oil to the marinade and mix well. Thread the chicken onto 12 metal skewers, alternating with the spring onions. Place skewers on the tray and brush generously with the marinade.
3 Grill the chicken

Chicken teriyaki (top), and Japanese pork and noodle stir-fry

under a hot grill for 2 minutes. Turn the skewers with tongs and brush with more marinade. Grill for a further 3–4 minutes, or until the chicken is cooked. Place the remaining marinade in a small saucepan over medium heat and bring to the boil. Serve the chicken with rice, and the marinade on the side.

Nutrition per serve: Fat 23 g; Protein 28 g; Carbohydrate 16 g; Dietary Fibre 0.5 g; Cholesterol 82.5 mg; 1670 kJ (400 Cal)

JAPANESE PORK AND NOODLE STIR-FRY
Ready to eat in 30 minutes
Serves 4

350 g pork fillet
1/3 cup (80 ml) soy sauce
1/4 cup (60 ml) mirin
2 teaspoons grated fresh
  ginger
2 cloves garlic, crushed
11/2 tablespoons soft brown
  sugar
500 g Hokkien noodles
2 tablespoons peanut oil
1 onion, cut into thin
  wedges
1 red capsicum, cut into thin
  strips
2 carrots, finely sliced on the
  diagonal
4 spring onions, finely sliced
  on the diagonal
200 g fresh shiitake
  mushrooms, sliced

1 Trim the pork of any excess fat or sinew and slice thinly. Combine the soy sauce, mirin, ginger, garlic and sugar in a large non-metallic bowl, add the pork and coat. Cover with plastic wrap and refrigerate for 10 minutes.
2 Meanwhile, place the noodles in a large bowl of hot water for 5 minutes to separate and soften.
3 Heat a large wok over high heat, add 1 tablespoon oil and swirl to coat. Drain the pork, reserving the marinade, and stir-fry in batches for 3 minutes, or until browned. Remove and keep warm.
4 Reheat the wok over high heat, add the remaining oil and swirl to coat. Add the onion, capsicum and carrot, and stir-fry for 2–3 minutes, or until just tender, then add the spring onion and shiitake mushrooms. Cook for another 2 minutes, then return the pork to the wok. Drain the noodles and add to the wok with the reserved marinade. Toss to combine and cook for another 1 minute, or until heated through, then serve.

Nutrition per serve: Fat 33 g; Protein 35 g; Carbohydrate 79 g; Dietary Fibre 13 g; Cholesterol 90.5 mg; 3160 kJ (755 Cal)

MUSHROOM AND WATER CHESTNUT STIR-FRY
Ready to eat in 25 minutes
Serves 4

1/4 cup (60 ml) oil
2 cloves garlic, julienned
1/2 cup (80 g) pine nuts
750 g mixed fresh mushrooms (e.g. Swiss brown, oyster, shiitake), sliced
100 g snow peas, halved
230 g can sliced water chestnuts, drained
150 g bean sprouts
1/3 cup (80 ml) oyster sauce
2 teaspoons sesame oil

1 Heat a wok over high heat, add 2 tablespoons oil and swirl until the wok is coated. Add the garlic and pine nuts, and cook, stirring constantly, for 1 minute, or until light golden brown.
2 Add the mushrooms and stir-fry over high heat for 3 minutes. Add the snow peas and cook for a further 3 minutes, or until the vegetables are just tender, adding the remaining oil, if necessary.
3 Add the water chestnuts, bean sprouts, oyster sauce and sesame oil, and cook for a further 30 seconds. Serve with rice.

Nutrition per serve: Fat 31.5 g; Protein 13 g; Carbohydrate 16 g; Dietary Fibre 9 g; Cholesterol 0 mg; 1645 kJ (395 Cal)

Note: If you are watching your weight, omit the pine nuts from this recipe.

SALMON WITH CUCUMBER COLESLAW
Ready to eat in 30 minutes
Serves 4

1 Lebanese cucumber
200 g green cabbage, sliced thinly
1/3 cup (80 ml) rice wine vinegar, plus 1 tablespoon extra
2 teaspoons sugar, plus 1/3 cup (90 g) extra
1/4 cup (60 ml) fish sauce
4 spring onions, thinly sliced
1 teaspoon sambal oelek
4 x 200 g salmon fillets
1 tablespoon oil
1/2 cup (15 g) loosely packed fresh coriander leaves

1 Cut the cucumber in half lengthways. Remove the seeds with a teaspoon and cut the flesh into very thin slices on the diagonal. Place in a large bowl with the cabbage.
2 Combine the vinegar, sugar and 1 teaspoon salt in a small saucepan. Simmer until the sugar and salt dissolve. Cool slightly then pour over the cucumber and cabbage and refrigerate.
3 Place the extra sugar and 2 tablespoons water in a small, heavy-based saucepan. Cook over medium heat for 5 minutes, shaking the pan occasionally, until the sugar melts and turns golden brown. Remove from the heat and add the fish sauce (be careful as it will splatter), remaining vinegar, spring onion and sambal oelek.
4 Season the salmon lightly with salt. Heat a large heavy-based frying pan over medium heat, add the oil, and then add the salmon and cook on one side for 1 minute, or until browned. Turn over and cook the other side for 1 minute. Reduce the heat to medium and add the sauce. Turn the salmon to coat thoroughly in the glaze.
5 Add the coriander to the cabbage mixture, toss to combine and season to taste. Place the salmon on top of the coleslaw and serve with boiled rice.

Nutrition per serve: Fat 19 g; Protein 42 g; Carbohydrate 28 g; Dietary Fibre 3 g; Cholesterol 104 mg; 1875 kJ (450 Cal)

Mushroom and water chestnut stir-fry (top), and Salmon with cucumber coleslaw

Index